WHERE'S MY GROOVE?

📞 ⫘⫘God Talk

WHERE'S MY GROOVE?

God Talk

Editing and Production Team:
Gregory C. Benoit, James F. Couch, Jr.,
Katharine Harris, Scott Lee

SERENDIPITY
HOUSE

NASHVILLE, TN

Published by Serendipity House Publishers
Nashville, Tennessee

International Standard Book Number: 1-57494-116-X

Dewey Decimal Classification: 248.83
Subject Heading: God-Will/Christian Life—Questions and Answers

ACKNOWLEDGMENTS

Scripture quotations are taken from the
Holman Christian Standard Bible,
© Copyright 2000 by Holman Bible Publishers. Used by permission.

To Zondervan Bible Publishers for permission to use the NIV text,
The Holy Bible, New International Bible Society.
© 1973, 1978, 1984 by International Bible Society.
Used by permission of Zondervan Bible Publishers.

03 04 05 06 07 08 / 10 9 8 7 6 5 4 3 2 1

Nashville, Tennessee
1-800-525-9563
www.serendipityhouse.com

TABLE OF
CONTENTS

SERENDIPITY

God Talk

All of us go through periods of wondering just where we fit in, what it is that we're meant to do. This questioning is more pronounced in our youth, a time when we tend to role-play who we're going to become someday.

But this question is not restricted to the young; it is something that most of us will ask ourselves from time to time throughout life. Therefore it is worthwhile to remember often what the Lord tells us our purpose in life should be.

WHAT THIS STUDY IS AND ISN'T

This is not a Bible study on the subject of spiritual gifts. That topic certainly comes into play in figuring out just what our roles are in life, but this is a more basic study than that.

The seven Bible studies contained in this book focus on the basics of understanding who we are as children of God. It addresses such issues as finding the real me, finding where I belong, being connected, and other pertinent topics related to "finding my groove."

Throughout these studies, however, a few major themes will emerge. The child of God is first and foremost just that: a child of the Almighty God. This in itself is a huge and very significant realization, and it is one which ought to color our understanding of who we are as people.

Further, we will see that our primary mission in life is to serve others, to look after the cares and concerns of one another. Our mission is actually two-directional, involving love for one another and worship of God.

WHAT WE'LL STUDY

These truths come to life for us as we read about real people living in the real world, people who found for themselves a basic understanding of what their "groove" was. It is sometimes easier to understand such abstract topics as this by imitating others, and the Scriptures are full of men and women who are worthy of our emulation.

In these seven studies, we will look at the woman (traditionally thought to be Mary Magdalene) who washes Jesus' feet with her tears, we will watch as Shadrack and his friends are thrown into the fiery furnace, we will see Joseph of Arimathea come openly to bury Jesus, and we will learn from their actions just what it means to be a child of the King.

In these studies, we will ask ourselves the questions of who we are and what we're supposed to do in life, and we'll find answers in the lives of the saints. We will find out first-hand where our groove is.

ACTIVITIES

This is the hands-on stuff, the opening activity that gets the group laughing together and helps them feel comfortable. There are generally two activity ideas. These ideas can also help to suggest your own ideas for activities that you create.

ICEBREAKERS

This is the "icebreaker" section, the transition time from entertaining activity toward more serious discussion. It normally offers three icebreaker questions which are very general in nature and help the group to move toward a serious consideration of God's Word.

SCRIPTURE READING

A Scripture passage is given, and the text is included for convenience. (Because the reading is usually broken into parts for several group members to read, you may copy the Scripture text for each member of the group.)

DISCUSSION QUESTIONS

This section digs into the Bible study. The Scripture passage is followed by four to six probing questions in two different categories which encourage the group to look closely at what God's Word has to say on the topic of discussion. There are two types of questions here: factual, interpretive (or "head") questions which help the group to understand the passage; and practical, application (or "heart") questions that ask the group members to consider how they will put the ideas into practice in their own lives.

CARING TIME

The "feet" of any philosophical study is the act of putting ideas into practice. In this final section the leader will find some suggestions on possible questions to ask of the group, questions that will urge each person to plan on putting into practice the ideas that have been studied. It is essential that the group spend some time in prayer during this portion of the meeting. At times suggestions will be offered to guide the prayer. Make sure you are sensitive to the concerns that the group members share during the discussions. Incorporate these concerns into the prayer time.

NEXT WEEK

Each study concludes with an overview of what will be studied in the next session. This also includes a "heads up," a note to the leader of anything that may require any advanced preparation, such as things to ask the group members to bring with them next week.

NOTES.

Finally, additional notes are provided which will assist the leader in understanding such issues as the culture in which the story is taking place, background on the people in the story, and points to consider in directing the discussion.

STUDY 01

Finding the Real Me

LUKE 7:36-50

We all have times where we feel that we just don't fit in, don't have much to offer. Sometimes we just feel inferior to others who seem to have more talents or resources, who seem able to do things effortlessly where we struggle just to get started.

The problem is that we tend to look at man's accomplishments as being very significant, as though we define who we are by what we accomplish. Man looks on the outward appearance, but God looks on the heart. He is more interested in who we are than in what we accomplish.

A perfect example of this is found in today's passage, where Jesus spends an evening with a law-abiding Pharisee and a reformed prostitute. The Pharisee would be a man of accomplishment; the ex-prostitute a woman of contrite spirit. She had nothing to offer Jesus but her repentance and worship, yet she ends up serving Him best. In our opening study, we will learn that God wants His children to love Him above all else.

ACTIVITIES

Choose one of the activities below.

FOOT WASH OR NOT Have a group of 4-8 lie down on the ground with their feet in the air. Balance a bucket full of water on their up turned feet. The object is for everyone to remove their shoes without spilling the water.

BALLOON POP RELAY Divide into two teams with each member having a deflated balloon. Each has to run from the starting line to a chair, blow up the balloon, pop it by sitting on it, and return to the starting line to tag the next in line.

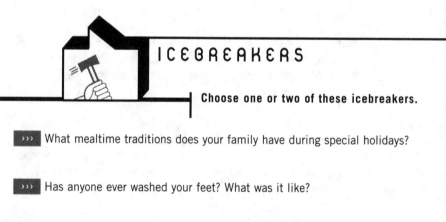

ICEBREAKERS

Choose one or two of these icebreakers.

>>> What mealtime traditions does your family have during special holidays?

>>> Has anyone ever washed your feet? What was it like?

>>> What is your favorite perfume or cologne? Why?

SCRIPTURE READING

Read Luke 7:36-50

READER ONE: ³⁶ Then one of the Pharisees invited Him to eat with him. He entered the Pharisee's house and reclined at the table. ³⁷ And a woman in the town who was a sinner found out that Jesus was reclining at the table in the Pharisee's house. She brought an alabaster flask of fragrant oil ³⁸ and stood behind Him at His feet, weeping, and began to wash His feet with her tears. She wiped His feet with the hair of her head, kissing them and anointing them with the fragrant oil.

READER TWO: ³⁹ When the Pharisee who had invited Him saw this, he said to himself, "This man, if He were a prophet, would know who and what kind of woman this is who is touching Him—that she's a sinner!"
⁴⁰ Jesus replied to him, "Simon, I have something to say to you." "Teacher," he said, "say it."

READER THREE: ⁴¹ "A creditor had two debtors. One owed 500 denarii, and the other 50. ⁴² Since they could not pay it back, he graciously forgave them both. So, which of them will love him more?" ⁴³ Simon answered, "I suppose the one he forgave more."
"You have judged correctly," He told him. ⁴⁴ Turning to the woman, He said to Simon, "Do you see this woman? I entered your house; you gave Me no water for My feet, but she, with her tears, has washed My feet and wiped them with her hair. ⁴⁵ You gave Me no kiss, but she hasn't stopped kissing My feet since I came in. ⁴⁶ You didn't anoint My head with oil, but she has anointed My feet with fragrant oil. ⁴⁷ Therefore I tell you, her many sins have been forgiven; that's why she loved much. But the one who is forgiven little, loves little." ⁴⁸ Then He said to her, "Your sins are forgiven."

READER FOUR: ⁴⁹ Those who were at the table with Him began to say among themselves, "Who is this man who even forgives sins?"
⁵⁰ And He said to the woman, "Your faith has saved you. Go in peace."

Luke 7:36–50

DISCUSSION QUESTIONS

Select four or five questions from the head
and heart sections, and/or make up your own.

>>> This woman had probably been a prostitute. Why does she come to Jesus?

>>> What does this woman do for Jesus? What is her motivation?

>>> It was customary for a servant to wash a guest's feet before dinner, and honored guests would be anointed with oil. Why does Simon fail to do these things?

>>> What does Jesus mean when he says "one who is forgiven little, loves little" (v. 47)?

>>> How does the Pharisee show that he loves Jesus very little?

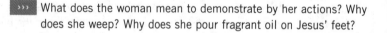

>>> What does the woman mean to demonstrate by her actions? Why does she weep? Why does she pour fragrant oil on Jesus' feet?

>>> In what ways is this woman's service for Jesus more significant than the Pharisee's?

>>> Simon was probably a fairly influential man. If he'd loved Jesus more, how might he have been of service to Him?

>>> Why does Jesus tell Simon this parable? Do you think that Simon was less of a sinner than the former prostitute? Why or why not?

>>> How does Simon's attitude compare with the woman's? How does her attitude prepare her to be of real service to Jesus?

CARING TIME

Use these questions and/or make up your own.

››› Has Jesus forgiven you a little, a lot, or somewhere between? How much do you love Him in return?

››› Who do you think pleased Jesus more—Simon or the woman? Who are you most like?

››› Spend time as a group worshiping Jesus, thanking Him for His forgiveness.

NEXT WEEK

This week we learned from the woman who sat at Jesus' feet just what things are really important in life, and what things are not so important. In the coming week, make it a point each day to spend a few minutes worshiping God and thanking Him for His love and forgiveness. Next week we will meet Samuel and learn how he figured out where he belonged.

NOTES ON LUKE 7,36-50

37 a sinner. This is probably a delicate way of saying that this woman had been the town's prostitute. She would be at the opposite end of the social scale from a Pharisee. She'd have less money, education, and influence, the sort of person who has little to contribute to society.

38 weeping. The woman carried a jar made of alabaster containing fragrant oil. She had to actually break the jar in order to pour out its fragrant contents, a good symbol of her love and worship. She had to voluntarily let her heart be broken in grief over her own sin, before the true fragrance of devotion and gratitude could pour forth. Simon's heart seems too hard to be broken that way.

41 denarii. One denarius was the common daily wage for laborers. So one man owes a month and a half of salary, the other a year and a half. Both men are heavily in debt.

44 you gave Me no water. Customarily, the host would greet his guest with a kiss on the cheek, offering him water to wash his feet. A wealthy host would have a servant washing feet, and an honored guest would be anointed with fragrant oil. Simon's lack of courtesy suggests that he's rather unimpressed with who Jesus is.

47 loves little. Simon's problem seems to be his own arrogance—he does not realize that he needs Jesus' forgiveness. This lack of repentance and gratitude to God prevents him from being of any service to Jesus whatsoever. It is ironic that the one with the most potential from the world's perspective is of least service, while the one with the least to offer serves Jesus best.

STUDY 02

Finding Where I Belong

1 SAMUEL 3:1-21

It is quite natural, especially when we are young, to wonder from time to time just where we fit in. What job am I to do? What's my purpose, my calling?

Young Samuel had a calling—literally. It came to him when he was a youth, one who didn't know about God. This in itself helps us to see one important point: that it is God who does the calling, it is God who will tell each of His children how to serve Him. Also, what we know and what we're trained in is quite secondary. God took a boy who knew nothing and used him as one of His greatest prophets.

This week we will discover that we all fit into God's body; it is up to each one of us to obey His call.

ACTIVITIES

Choose one of the activities below.

STUMP THE WISE GUY Select two know-it-all's from the group. Then have each person there write out a philosophical question on a 3 x 5 card (don't allow questions with yes or no answers or those that require specific factual answers). An example would be, "Why do women feel more comfortable talking about their feelings than men?" Give each of the Wise Guys a loaded water pistol and have them sit facing one another. Shuffle the questions and begin alternating between the two, asking questions. When the one being asked hesitates the other may fire away. The question is answered when the leader says something like "thank you," "next question," or "moving on."

HIDE AND SQUEEZE One person is "it" and is given one minute to hide. When someone finds "it" that person must squeeze into the same hiding place. Continue until the last person finds "it."

ICEBREAKERS

Choose one or two of these icebreakers.

››› Do you ever walk in your sleep? What is the funniest experience you've had?

››› How old were you when you first learned about God? Who taught you?

››› Are you a light sleeper or a sound sleeper? Do you remember your dreams?

SCRIPTURE READING

Read the following passages from the 1 Samuel 3:1-21.

READER ONE: ¹ The boy Samuel ministered before the LORD under Eli. In those days the word of the LORD was rare; there were not many visions. ² One night Eli, whose eyes were becoming so weak that he could barely see, was lying down in his usual place. ³ The lamp of God had not yet gone out, and Samuel was lying down in the temple of the LORD , where the ark of God was. ⁴ Then the LORD called Samuel.

READER TWO: Samuel answered, "Here I am." ⁵ And he ran to Eli and said, "Here I am; you called me." But Eli said, "I did not call; go back and lie down." So he went and lay down. ⁶ Again the LORD called, "Samuel!" And Samuel got up and went to Eli and said, "Here I am; you called me." "My son," Eli said, "I did not call; go back and lie down."

READER THREE: ⁷ Now Samuel did not yet know the LORD : The word of the LORD had not yet been revealed to him. ⁸ The LORD called Samuel a third time, and Samuel got up and went to Eli and said, "Here I am; you called me." Then Eli realized that the LORD was calling the boy. ⁹ So Eli told Samuel, "Go and lie down, and if he calls you, say, 'Speak, LORD , for your servant is listening.' " So Samuel went and lay down in his place.

READER FOUR: ¹⁰ The LORD came and stood there, calling as at the other times, "Samuel! Samuel!" Then Samuel said, "Speak, for your servant is listening." ¹¹ And the LORD said to Samuel: "See, I am about to do something in Israel that will make the ears of everyone who hears of it tingle. ¹² At that time I will carry out against Eli everything I spoke against his family—from beginning to end. ¹³ For I told him that I would judge his family forever because of the sin he knew about; his sons made themselves contemptible, and he failed to restrain them. ¹⁴ Therefore, I swore to the house of Eli, 'The guilt of Eli's house will never be atoned for by sacrifice or offering.' "

READER FIVE. ¹⁵ Samuel lay down until morning and then opened the doors of the house of the LORD . He was afraid to tell Eli the vision, ¹⁶ but Eli called him and said, "Samuel, my son."

Samuel answered, "Here I am." ¹⁷ "What was it he said to you?" Eli asked. "Do not hide it from me. May God deal with you, be it ever so severely, if you hide from me anything he told you." ¹⁸ So Samuel told him everything, hiding nothing from him. Then Eli said, "He is the LORD; let him do what is good in his eyes."

READER ONE. ¹⁹ The LORD was with Samuel as he grew up, and he let none of his words fall to the ground. ²⁰ And all Israel from Dan to Beersheba recognized that Samuel was attested as a prophet of the LORD . ²¹ The LORD continued to appear at Shiloh, and there he revealed himself to Samuel through his word.

1 Samuel 3:1–21

DISCUSSION QUESTIONS

Select four or five questions from the head and heart sections, and/or make up your own.

>>> Why did young Samuel think that Eli was calling him?

>>> Why do you think that God didn't speak more to Samuel until Samuel knew who it was that was calling him? Why did Samuel need to address God instead of Eli?

>>> Why was Samuel afraid to tell Eli what God said? Why didn't he soften God's painful words when he did tell Eli?

>>> What was Samuel's job as a boy? What did he become?

>>> What does it mean that Samuel "let none of [Gods'] words fall to the ground" (v. 19)? How did his first encounter with God demonstrate this?

>>> If you had been Samuel, how would you have reacted to hearing your name called three times? Would you have bothered getting up the third time?

>>> What skills did Samuel have when God first called him? Where did he get his training as he grew up?

>>> Who gave Samuel his "calling" in life? Samuel? Eli? God? Who was responsible for obeying that calling?

>>> What was Samuel's basic attitude toward God's word? What was his attitude toward taking orders?

>>> God generally does not wake us up to tell us what we're to be when we grow up. How are we to figure that out? How can we be like Samuel in that process?

CARING TIME

Use these questions and/or make up your own.

>>> What is your attitude toward taking orders? How teachable are you?

>>> Do you ever let God's words fall to the ground? What part of His words do you need to hold on to?

>>> What do you think God wants you to be learning right now? To be doing?

NEXT WEEK

This week we watched as Samuel spoke with God and learned what his calling was to be in life. This week, ask the Lord to give you a teachable spirit like Samuel's, that He might be able to show you His will for your life. Next week we will discover what makes each of us unique.

1 The boy Samuel. Samuel was probably around 12 years old at this point. (For complete background, read 1 Samuel 1 and 2.) His job seems to be fairly menial—the personal servant of Eli, responsible for such tasks as opening the temple doors in the morning (v. 15). He had no real knowledge of God—a poor reflection on Eli the high priest—and the Lord's visitations were rare, so Samuel had little prospect at this point for any great role in God's service.

4 Samuel answered. This was part of Samuel's secret to success: he always responded when God called. In other words, Samuel was obedient. He was faithful in doing unglamorous jobs in the temple, and therefore proved faithful to greater tasks later. This early training in obedience and faithfulness was very important for Samuel—and for all of us.

7 Samuel did not yet know the LORD. This is a very encouraging statement; it shows us that God will use all of us, even those who are least promising from man's perspective. God is always the One who initiates a relationship with men, calling us to salvation, and then leading us to the place of service.

9 your servant is listening. God does not force Himself or His will on any of His children. He wants each of us to be willing to listen and obey before He will reveal Himself. Samuel needed to understand just who he was speaking to—it was not Eli that was calling, it was not any man, but the Lord of Creation.

15 He was afraid to tell Eli. (See chapter 2 for background.) Samuel's task was very difficult—he must tell someone of God's coming judgment. But Samuel learned from this experience that he must be faithful to obey what God commands, and to obey fully.

19 he let none of his words fall to the ground. Samuel treasured God's Word, clinging to it to obey it. This was the key to his success in his calling, since the people around him learned that he had God's true Word. It is also at the core of any Christian's calling, whatever the task may be.

STUDY 03

Finding What Makes Me Different

SELECTIONS FROM ESTHER 2-4

Every believer in Christ is a unique member of His body, each fulfilling a unique role. Just as God designed hands and feet differently in order to do different jobs, so also He prepares each of His children in different ways to serve the body best.

Esther is a good example of this. She was a Jew who lived in a foreign land, in a culture that was very different from her own. God placed her—through no effort or planning of her own—in a place where she would save the entire Jewish nation from extinction.

What made Esther different, from a human perspective, was that she was beautiful. However, there were many other beautiful women besides Esther, and what made her different from God's perspective was a willingness to obey, even at great risk. This week we will meet Esther and see how she discovered what made her different.

ACTIVITIES

Choose one of the activities below.

CLOTHESPINS You will need at least five clothespins for every person present. Give an equal number to everyone. When told to start the players have three minutes to pin others with the five clothespins provided, plus any pinned on them. The player with the least number of attached clothespins wins.

COUNT OFF Have the group seated, preferably on the floor and in a random pattern. The group must count off from one to the total number of people playing within the prescribed time period (one second for each of the total number playing). The leader will select someone in the middle of the group to start. No talking or gesturing is allowed. If the group can't make through in the time allowed or two people say the same number, start again.

ICEBREAKERS

Choose one or two of these icebreakers.

››› If you won an "inner beauty" contest, what would your title be? Miss Patience? Mr. Peace? Ms. Self-control?

››› Have you ever fasted? For how long? What was it like?

››› If you were king or queen for a day, what would you do?

SCRIPTURE READING

**Read the following passages
from Esther 2–4**

Esther 2

READER ONE ² Then the king's personal attendants proposed, "Let a search be made for beautiful young virgins for the king. ³ Let the king appoint commissioners in every province of his realm to bring all these beautiful girls into the harem at the citadel of Susa. ... ⁴ Then let the girl who pleases the king be queen instead of Vashti." This advice appealed to the king, and he followed it.

READER TWO ⁵ Now there was in the citadel of Susa a Jew of the tribe of Benjamin, named Mordecai ... ⁷ Mordecai had a cousin named Hadassah, whom he had brought up because she had neither father nor mother. This girl, who was also known as Esther, was lovely in form and features, and Mordecai had taken her as his own daughter when her father and mother died.

READER THREE ⁸ When the king's order and edict had been proclaimed, many girls were brought to the citadel of Susa and put under the care of Hegai. Esther also was taken to the king's palace and entrusted to Hegai, who had charge of the harem. ...

READER FOUR ¹⁰ Esther had not revealed her nationality and family background, because Mordecai had forbidden her to do so. ¹¹ Every day he walked back and forth near the courtyard of the harem to find out how Esther was and what was happening to her. ...¹⁷ Now the king was attracted to Esther more than to any of the other women, and she won his favor and approval more than any of the other virgins. So he set a royal crown on her head and made her queen instead of Vashti.

Esther 3

READER ONE ⁸ Then Haman said to King Xerxes, "There is a certain people dispersed and scattered among the peoples in all the provinces of your kingdom whose customs are different from those of all other people and who do not obey the king's laws; it is not in the king's best interest to tolerate them ⁹ If it pleases the king, let a decree be issued to destroy them, and I will put ten thousand talents of silver into the royal treasury for the men who carry out this business." ¹⁰ So the king took his signet ring from his finger and gave it to Haman son of Hammedatha, the Agagite, the enemy of the Jews. ...

Esther 4

READER TWO: [1] When Mordecai learned of all that had been done, he tore his clothes, put on sackcloth and ashes, and went out into the city, wailing loudly and bitterly. ... [4] When Esther's maids and eunuchs came and told her about Mordecai, she was in great distress. ... [5] Then Esther summoned Hathach, one of the king's eunuchs assigned to attend her, and ordered him to find out what was troubling Mordecai and why. ...

READER THREE: [12] When Esther's words were reported to Mordecai, [13] he sent back this answer: "Do not think that because you are in the king's house you alone of all the Jews will escape. [14] For if you remain silent at this time, relief and deliverance for the Jews will arise from another place, but you and your father's family will perish. And who knows but that you have come to royal position for such a time as this?"

READER FOUR: [15] Then Esther sent this reply to Mordecai: [16] "Go, gather together all the Jews who are in Susa, and fast for me. Do not eat or drink for three days, night or day. I and my maids will fast as you do. When this is done, I will go to the king, even though it is against the law. And if I perish, I perish."

Esther 2–4

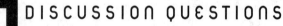

DISCUSSION QUESTIONS

Select four or five questions from the head and heart sections, and/or make up your own.

››› In what ways was Esther different from other people around her?

››› The king's harem had the most beautiful women from his entire kingdom. Why did he choose Esther to be his queen? What, besides her beauty, caused the king to look on her with favor?

››› Why did the king agree to kill all the Jews? How did their being different endanger them?

>>> Why did God make Esther queen?

>>> What risk did Esther take by protecting the Jews? Why did she take that risk?

 >>> If you'd been Esther, how would you have felt when you became queen? Would you feel that you deserved it?

>>> How would you have felt when you discovered that someone wanted to kill your people? What would you have done?

>>> How was Esther uniquely qualified to do the job that God wanted her to do? What had she done to prepare for it? What had God done to prepare her?

>>> How did Esther find out what her special job was? What would have happened if she hadn't obeyed?

>>> Since you don't know how God is preparing you for some future task, how can you best be preparing for it now?

CARING TIME

Use these questions and/or make up your own.

>>> What commands is God asking you to obey this week? What risk do you run by obeying? By disobeying?

>>> What people are you uniquely qualified to serve? How can you best serve them?

>>> What opportunities do you have this week to help people?

NEXT WEEK

This week we met Esther, a woman who was different from the people around her, and saw how God used that for His own glory. In the coming week, ask the Lord to help you see the things about you that are very special in His eyes, and then ask Him to teach you how to use your uniqueness in His service. Next week we will meet a man who learned how to use his own strengths to serve God.

NOTES ON ESTHER 2-4

2:4 let the girl who pleases the king be queen. (See chapter 1 for context.) God is never directly mentioned in this book. The author leaves it up to us to discover God's hand of sovereignty in the story. Read the whole book to see how God ordered the events in the lives of Esther and Mordecai, placing them in exactly the right places at the right moments, all the time preparing them to be His servants in saving the Jews. The author does not tell us that Esther pleased the king because God made it so, yet that is undoubtedly the truth.

2:10 Esther had not revealed her nationality. One of the things that made her different was her Jewish heritage and customs. It became very important later on that Haman did not know that she was Jewish. **because Mordecai had forbidden her.** This is the real thing that sets Esther apart: an obedient spirit. She's queen, after all—who is this Mordecai to forbid her anything? It would have been extremely easy for this power and honor to go to a young woman's head, but Esther continued to be loyal and teachable, looking to Mordecai for counsel.

3:8 whose customs are different. Haman falsely accused the Jews of violating the king's laws, when in fact it was only Mordecai who refused to bow down to Haman. The Jew's faithfulness to God's commandments set them apart from others. This will often make believers very different from the people around them.

4:13 because you are in the king's house. This is the point where Esther's true qualities shone forth. Another person might have forgotten that it was God's hand that had made her queen, or become so attached to the power and comfort that she'd be unwilling to risk losing it. But Esther had a habit of obeying and heeding counsel—that is what made her different.

16 if I perish, I perish. See chapter 1 to fully understand this. Esther took her life in her hands when she agreed to speak to the king.

STUDY 04

Finding Where I Can Be the Best

JOHN 19:38-42; MARK 15:42-46

Little is known of Joseph of Arimathea. He was a member of the Jewish ruling council that sentenced Christ to the cross, yet he himself argued on behalf of the Lord. Like Nicodemus, he seems to have been in fear of the powerful Jews, shunning any bold public discipleship.

However, after the Lord's crucifixion, Joseph came forward boldly and claimed Jesus' body for burial. To some, this may seem like second-rate service to the Lord, perhaps too little too late. Yet Joseph was serving Jesus in the way he could best, and in so doing he provided a service to the Lord that others could not have done. As wealthy men, he and Nicodemus gave generously of their gifts, offering the Lord a very costly burial, worthy of the King.

This week we will see that the Lord often uses our gifts and strengths to serve Him in ways that we would not expect.

ACTIVITIES

Choose one of the activities below.

TEAM TAG Have everyone but "it" line up on either side of the play area. When you say "cross," they must travel to the opposite side. When "it" tags someone, that person joins "it" in tagging. Continue crossing until only one person hasn't been tagged.

CIRCLE DANCE Make a number of separate circles with tape on the floor, enough so that everyone can fit within the circles marked. Have the group move in a larger circle around the room. When you say "stop," everyone must go to a circle. If they don't have both feet in the circle and both touching the floor they are out. Be careful to state the directions accurately. Each time remove a tape circle until they catch on that they don't have to stand in the circles to have both feet in the circle.

ICEBREAKERS

Choose one or two of these icebreakers.

›› What's your favorite material for clothes: linen, cotton, rayon, polyester, other?

›› If you could be a secret agent, what sort of espionage work would you do?

›› Who is the boldest person you know? What sort of bold deeds has he or she done?

SCRIPTURE READING

Read the following passages from

John 19:38-42; Mark 15:42-46

John 19

READER ONE ³⁸ After this, Joseph of Arimathea, who was a disciple of Jesus—but secretly because of his fear of the Jews—asked Pilate that he might remove Jesus' body. Pilate gave him permission, so he came and took His body away. ³⁹ Nicodemus (who had previously come to Him at night) also came, bringing a mixture of about 75 pounds of myrrh and aloes. ⁴⁰ Then they took Jesus' body and wrapped it in linen cloths with the aromatic spices, according to the burial custom of the Jews. ⁴¹ There was a garden in the place where He was crucified. And in the garden was a new tomb in which no one had yet been placed. ⁴² So because of the Jewish preparation day, since the tomb was nearby, they placed Jesus there.

Mark 15

READER TWO ⁴² When it was already evening, because it was preparation day (that is, the day before the Sabbath), ⁴³ Joseph of Arimathea, a prominent member of the Sanhedrin who was himself looking forward to the kingdom of God, came and boldly went in to Pilate and asked for Jesus' body. ⁴⁴ Pilate was surprised that He was already dead. Summoning the centurion, he asked him whether He had already died. ⁴⁵ When he found out from the centurion, he granted the corpse to Joseph. ⁴⁶ After he bought some fine linen, he took Him down and wrapped Him in the linen. Then he placed Him in a tomb cut out of the rock, and rolled a stone against the entrance to the tomb.

John 19:38–42; Mark 15:42–46

DISCUSSION QUESTIONS

Select four or five questions from the head and heart sections, and/or make up your own.

>>> Why was Joseph of Arimathea a "secret" disciple of Jesus? What did he fear?

>>> Why had Nicodemus "previously come to [Jesus] at night" (John 19:39)? If these two men were afraid to be seen with Jesus when alive, why are they being so bold now?

>>> Joseph was "a prominent member of the Sanhedrin" (Mark 15:43), the council that had sentenced Jesus to death. What risk was he taking here by burying the crucified Christ? Why did he take this risk?

>>> What does it mean that Joseph was "looking forward to the kingdom of God" (Mark 15:43)?

>>> In what way was Joseph serving the Lord here? Did his service matter? Why?

>>> Why did Joseph go "boldly" before Pilate? How did this compare with being a "secret disciple"?

>>> The burial that Joseph and Nicodemus gave the Lord is very expensive. Why was that appropriate for Christ? How was Joseph more able to do this than the disciples?

>>> Luke tells us that Joseph openly opposed the Sanhedrin's decision to crucify Jesus. How did Joseph actively use the gifts he had to serve Christ? In what ways was he not as well qualified to be one of the 12 apostles?

>>> What gifts has God given you: talents, resources, opportunities, etc? What kinds of service do these equip you for?

>>> What kinds of "secret discipleship" are not appropriate? How can you avoid these things?

CARING TIME

Use these questions and/or make up your own.

>>> Do you struggle with fears of being a bold disciple of Christ? How can this group help you be more bold?

>>> Are you using the gifts you have—time, money, talents—to serve God or yourself? How can you use your gifts better this week?

>>> Are you content to serve the Lord in unglamorous ways?

NEXT WEEK

This week we saw that Joseph of Arimathea found ways to serve the Lord that utilized the gifts he'd been given. In the coming week ask the Lord to help you see the many gifts He's given you, and look for ways to use those gifts to serve others. Next week we will meet two very close friends, and we will see how close friendship helps us to stay connected.

NOTES ON JOHN 19.38-42; MARK 15.42-46

John 19

38 secretly. Scripture does not condemn Joseph or Nicodemus for their fear of being bold for Christ. Joseph had legitimate reasons to be fearful, given his prominent role in the Sanhedrin. Nevertheless, the Lord ultimately does not want His people to be ashamed of the gospel, and both Joseph and Nicodemus come forward in these passages with boldness. Joseph still ran a high risk in asking for the body of Jesus, since he was openly identifying himself as a supporter of a condemned "outlaw."

39 Nicodemus. Nicodemus was a member of the ruling council, and he had spoken out in defense of Jesus. When he came to Jesus at night (John 3) it was because of fear of the Jews, yet he risked his fears to ask the Savior how to be born again. The Lord honors any amount of costly service; what seems cowardly to one man may be very brave for another. **75 pounds of myrrh.** The materials used for Jesus' burial, including the tomb, were very costly. Matthew tells us that Joseph was a rich man. Jesus tells us that it is very difficult for a rich man to enter the kingdom of heaven. Joseph is an example of a man who is using the gifts he's been given to serve the Lord, despite a struggle with his own desires for security and reputation.

Mark 15
43 prominent member of the Sanhedrin. The Sanhedrin was the Jewish ruling council that condemned Jesus to death. Joseph may well have risked being condemned to death as well by being overly bold in his discipleship. Mark tells us that everyone fled and abandoned Jesus when He was condemned, yet here we find Joseph coming forward "boldly" to give Jesus an honored burial. **looking forward to the kingdom of God.** Here is the central point: when push came to shove, Joseph's main desire was to serve God. Whether he lacked boldness or was just not able to give more openly, he proved that his greatest treasure was in heaven, not on earth.

STUDY 05

Being Connected

1 SAMUEL 20:1-42

An important aspect of figuring out who we are and where we fit in is realizing what it means to be part of the body of Christ. If we are part of the body, then obviously we must stay connected to the other parts.

What does it mean to be connected? Just how and why should we do it? A good example of "connectedness" is found in the relationship between Jonathan and David. These two men understood that they could not stand alone as safely as they could stand together.

As we will see in this story, being connected means being willing to sacrifice one-self for others; it means caring for one another through thick and thin. As David and Jonathan discovered, it is a vital part of serving God.

This week we will see how being connected can help us find our "groove."

ACTIVITIES

Choose one of the activities below.

COIN FLIP In groups of 4-6 have each person flip a nickle with the thumb against a wall. The person whose coin ends up closest to the wall wins. Then have the winners of the different groups flip for the grand champion.

CLEAN SWEEP Have a soft puck, made from a rolled up sock, and two brooms. Number each player in two teams of the same size. You should have two ones, two twos, etc. When you call a number the two with that number run to the center of the room and try to push the puck toward the other's goal (a chair). When you call out another number those with the brooms drop them and the next two run out. Team with the most points wins. Play until everyone has a chance to play.

ICEBREAKERS

Choose one or two of these icebreakers.

>>> Have you ever shot a bow and arrow? How accurate were you?

>>> When you were a kid, did you enjoy hide and seek? Were you usually first found, last found, or in the middle?

>>> Do you have a "best friend"? Who is it? How close are you?

SCRIPTURE READING

Read the following passage from 1 Samuel 20.

READER ONE: [1] Then David fled from Naioth at Ramah and went to Jonathan and asked, "What have I done? What is my crime? How have I wronged your father, that he is trying to take my life?" [2] "Never!" Jonathan replied. "You are not going to die! Look, my father doesn't do anything, great or small, without confiding in me. Why would he hide this from me? It's not so!"

READER TWO: [3] But David took an oath and said, "Your father knows very well that I have found favor in your eyes, and he has said to himself, 'Jonathan must not know this or he will be grieved.' Yet as surely as the LORD lives and as you live, there is only a step between me and death." [4] Jonathan said to David, "Whatever you want me to do, I'll do for you."

READER THREE: [5] So David said, ... [8] "As for you, show kindness to your servant, for you have brought him into a covenant with you before the LORD. If I am guilty, then kill me yourself! Why hand me over to your father?" ...

READER FOUR: [16] So Jonathan made a covenant with the house of David, saying, "May the LORD call David's enemies to account." [17] And Jonathan had David reaffirm his oath out of love for him, because he loved him as he loved himself. [18] Then Jonathan said to David: ... [19] "The day after tomorrow, toward evening, go to the place where you hid when this trouble began, and wait by the stone Ezel. [20] I will shoot three arrows to the side of it, as though I were shooting at a target. [21] Then I will send a boy and say, 'Go, find the arrows.' If I say to him, 'Look, the arrows are on this side of you; bring them here,' then come, because, as surely as the LORD lives, you are safe; there is no danger. [22] But if I say to the boy, 'Look, the arrows are beyond you,' then you must go, because the LORD has sent you away. [23] And about the matter you and I discussed—remember, the LORD is witness between you and me forever." ...

READER ONE: [30] Saul's anger flared up at Jonathan and he said to him, "You son of a perverse and rebellious woman! Don't I know that you have sided with the son of Jesse to your own shame and to the shame of the mother who bore you? [31] As long as the son of Jesse lives on this earth, neither you nor your kingdom will be established. Now send and bring him to me, for he must die!" ³² "Why should he be put to death? What has he done?" Jonathan asked his father. ³³ But Saul hurled his spear at him to kill him. Then Jonathan knew that his father intended to kill David. ...

READER TWO: ³⁵ In the morning Jonathan went out to the field for his meeting with David. He had a small boy with him, ³⁶ and he said to the boy, "Run and find the arrows I shoot." As the boy ran, he shot an arrow beyond him. ³⁷ When the boy came to the place where Jonathan's arrow had fallen, Jonathan called out after him, "Isn't the arrow beyond you?" ³⁸ Then he shouted, "Hurry! Go quickly! Don't stop!" ...

READER THREE: ⁴¹ After the boy had gone, David got up from the south side of the stone and bowed down before Jonathan three times, with his face to the ground. Then they kissed each other and wept together—but David wept the most. ⁴² Jonathan said to David, "Go in peace, for we have sworn friendship with each other in the name of the LORD, saying, 'The LORD is witness between you and me, and between your descendants and my descendants forever.' " Then David left, and Jonathan went back to the town.

1 Samuel 20:1-42

DISCUSSION QUESTIONS

Select four or five questions from the head and heart sections, and/or make up your own.

>>> What problems was David facing? Why did he turn to Jonathan for help?

>>> Why did David even need help? Why couldn't he take care of his problems himself?

>>> What did Jonathan risk by helping David? What did he stand to gain?

>>> What was Jonathan's motive in helping David? How did his actions show real love for him?

What was the oath that the two friends swore together?

 How, in practical terms, can Christians show this kind of friendship for one another nowadays?

Why do Christians even need to have such friendships? Why is this important?

Describe the sort of person who would be like Jonathan in your life. Do you have any friends like that?

Do you know anyone who might need a "Jonathan friend"? How could you be that friend?

What difference in your own life would it make to have this kind of friendship? To offer this kind of friendship to someone else?

CARING TIME

Use these questions and/or make up your own.

Are you facing some big problems right now that need a "Jonathan's" help? How can this group become like Jonathan for you?

Is there someone you know who needs your help? Is that help going to be costly for you?

What things in your own life (fears, desires, priorities) make it hard for you to be an unselfish friend? How can this group help?

ΠΕΧΤ ШΕΕΚ

This week we saw the importance of being connected to other Christians. In the coming week, ask the Lord to show you ways that you can be like Jonathan for other people; in the process, you may well end up with a friend for yourself. Next week, we will meet the author of the Gospel of Mark, and discover that he wasn't always a great success.

1 David fled. Saul has already tried to kill David, and his life is very much in danger. Jonathan is Saul's son, and he takes a great risk in helping David. Furthermore, he is put in a difficult predicament, torn between loyalties to father, friend, and future career. Jonathan risks more than just his life; he also knows that, if David succeeds, he will take Jonathan's place on the throne. Jonathan sacrifices all he has and will have in order to help his friend, and he stands to gain nothing in return.

2 It's not so! Jonathan, however, does not undertake this agreement lightly. Part of being "connected" is to help one another understand truth, and Jonathan first sets out to make sure that David's concerns are well founded.

8 covenant. While swearing oaths of friendship is not the norm in our culture, we are still commanded to love one another to the point of sacrifice. A person who is well "connected" will be a person who learns to be loyal and unselfish to his brothers and sisters.

17 he loved him as he loved himself. This is the core of this week's study. The Jonathan-friend is the person who strives to obey the Lord's command to "love others as you love yourself." Jonathan's actions show what this means: setting the interests and needs above your own, even to the point of sacrificing all. The modern concept of "love yourself" is not found in Jonathan.

33 Saul hurled his spear at him. Jonathan's deep friendship for David, his commitment of love, has caused him to take on David's concerns quite literally. Jonathan's own life is now in danger, yet he will not abandon his friend.

42 in the name of the LORD. Being connected to other Christians really is not an option, it is a command. Jesus commanded us to love one another and to bear one another's burdens, and it is an important part of finding our place in life.

STUDY 06

Having a Mission

MARK 14:51,52; ACTS 12:25; 13:5,13; 15:36-40;
COLOSSIANS 4:10; 2 TIMOTHY 4:11

Finding where we fit in is actually a process, one involving failure and setback from time to time. This is especially true for young people who are seeking to discover their unique place in the body of Christ. Most of us will fall short of where we'd like to be at times.
The good news is that God gives second chances, and that He does not give up on us even if everyone else does.

John Mark provides us with a good example of this. Little is known of him from Scripture, but it is assumed that he is the author of the Gospel of Mark. This man, who wrote one of the Gospels, who traveled on missionary journeys with Paul and Barnabas, who learned about Jesus directly from Peter, had an inauspicious beginning to his career.

Ultimately, we will see that our mission in life is to serve others. This week we will see that having a mission may include a process of learning and growing, of failing and succeeding.

ACTIVITIES

Choose one of the activities below.

FRUIT BASKET RELAY Have two identical groups of fruit. Divide into two teams and give them a couple of minutes to strategize. They are to pass each piece of fruit down the line and back, before the next can be passed. They can't use the same method to pass the fruit from person to person twice (such as using their feet or chins or hands). First to complete the task wins.

INDOOR 4-SQUARE BALLOON BALL Divide the group into four teams seated on the floor. String rope from the tops of chairs to make a 4 square court with sheets draped over the rope. Use a balloon to play 4-square volleyball. Last team to return the balloon wins the point and serves the next point. Any team that breaks the balloon loses a point. First team to 11 wins.

ICEBREAKERS

Choose one or two of these icebreakers.

>>> Have you ever traveled outside the United States? Where? When?

>>> In what subject are you most likely to fail a pop quiz? Least likely?

>>> What skill have you learned through lots of practice? How long did it take you to become fairly competent?

SCRIPTURE READING

**Read the following passages from
Mark, Acts, Colossians, and 2 Timothy**

Mark 14 and Acts 12

READER ONE: 51 Now a certain young man, having a linen cloth wrapped around his naked body, was following Him. And they caught hold of him. 52 But he left the linen cloth behind and ran away naked. ...
25 And Barnabas and Saul returned to Jerusalem after they had completed their relief mission, on which they took John Mark.

Acts 13

READER TWO: 5 Arriving in Salamis, they proclaimed God's message in the Jewish synagogues. They also had John [Mark] as their assistant. ... 13 Paul and his companions set sail from Paphos and came to Perga in Pamphylia. John [Mark], however, left them and went back to Jerusalem.

Acts 15

READER THREE: 36 After some time had passed, Paul said to Barnabas, "Let's go back and visit the brothers in every town where we have preached the message of the Lord, and see how they're doing." 37 Barnabas wanted to take along John Mark. 38 But Paul did not think it appropriate to take along this man who had deserted them in Pamphylia and had not gone on with them to the work. 39 There was such a sharp disagreement that they parted company, and Barnabas took Mark with him and sailed off to Cyprus. 40 Then Paul chose Silas and departed, after being commended to the grace of the Lord by the brothers.

Colossians 4

READER FOUR: 10 Aristarchus, my fellow prisoner, greets you, as does [John] Mark, Barnabas' cousin (concerning whom you have received instructions: if he comes to you, welcome him),

2 Timothy 4

READER FIVE: 11 Only Luke is with me. Bring [John] Mark with you, for he is useful to me in the ministry.

Mark 14:51,52; Acts 12:25; 13:5,13; 15:36–40; Colossians 4:10; 2 Timothy 4:11

DISCUSSION QUESTIONS

Select four or five questions from the head and heart sections, and/or make up your own.

>>> John Mark, also called John and Mark, traveled briefly with Paul and Barnabas on their world-wide missionary journey. If you'd been in his place, why might you have quit and gone home midway, as Mark did?

>>> Why does Paul argue against letting Mark travel with them the second time (Acts 15:38)? If you'd been Paul, what would you have done?

>>> Why does Barnabas want to take Mark? If you'd been Mark, how would you have felt?

>>> Whose decision—Paul's or Barnabas'—do you think was better? Why?

>>> How does Paul's opinion of Mark change over time? Why?

>>> How might Mark's failure on the first missionary journey (Acts 13:13) have permanently damaged his ministry in life? Why doesn't it? How does Mark overcome that failure?

>>> What exactly is Mark's mission? What does he do?

>>> Mark eventually wrote the Gospel of Mark. How does his work with Paul and Barnabas prepare him for that task?

>>> How can failure sometimes help us to succeed in the future? What is required of us to turn failure into success?

>>> What is the true mission of all Christians? Give practical examples of ways that this group can fulfill their mission.

CARING TIME

Use these questions and/or make up your own.

>>> Have you failed in some area of life recently? How will you get back up and try again?

>>> Is there someone who has given you a second chance? Do you need to give someone else a second chance?

>>> How are you doing at serving others? How can this group serve people in our community?

NEXT WEEK

This week we discovered that even the great heroes of the faith have failed from time to time, but that a determination to keep striving for godliness can overcome failure. In the coming week, make it your top priority to overcome any areas where you have experienced failure. Next week, we will meet three friends who were absolutely sure of God's love, and it kept them cool in a heated time.

NOTES ON MARK 14:51,52; ACTS 12:25, 13:5,13; 15:36-40; COLOSSIANS 4:10, 2 TIMOTHY 4:11

Mark
14:51–52 Obviously no one can be sure that this young man is John Mark himself, yet it is traditionally believed to be the author's oblique reference to himself, much as John refers to himself as "the disciple whom Jesus loved."

Acts
12:25 It appears that John Mark accompanied Paul and Barnabas on at least part of their journeys, if not for one complete trip.

13:5 as their assistant. Mark's role was probably that of a servant. He was most likely not preaching or carrying out any of the up-front ministry such as Paul and Barnabas did, but was traveling with them as their servant or personal assistant. For some young people, this is a difficult role to fill; youthful zeal desires to get into the most dramatic or skilled tasks as quickly as possible, growing impatient with any lesser roles. Yet this was Mark's mission, to be the servant of the ministers of the gospel, and it was a very important function.

13:13 left them. There has been much speculation as to why Mark quit mid-way, including homesickness, a quarrel between Paul and Barnabas, and other surmising. Whatever the reason, it is clear that Mark quit early. This lends more weight to the idea that he is the same young man in Mark 14 who ran away at Christ's arrest. The young Mark, apparently, was a quitter, perhaps even overly timid.

15:37 Barnabas wanted ... Mark. Barnabas was a friend much like Jonathan—loyal and steadfast. Of course, he was also Mark's cousin, so kinship may have played a part here. But Barnabas was willing to give Mark another chance, and in the long run his patient mentoring paid off.

15:38 Paul did not think it appropriate. Paul's view was not wrong. He was in a position of needing to make wise decisions of leadership, and he did not do anything sinful in his decision. Nevertheless, his later relationship with Mark shows how highly Paul came to respect his helpful servant's heart.

Colossians
4:10 Evidently Mark was with Paul during some of Paul's imprisonment. It is quite possible that he was serving as Paul's secretary, helping him write some of his letters to the churches. By the end of Paul's life he became very important to the apostle, even as a son to him, proving how God works to make victors out of quitters.

STUDY 07

Being Sure

DANIEL 3:1-28

The question of where we fit in is, in the final analysis, not dependent upon our own efforts as much as it is upon the grace and power of God. Our job is to obey Him and serve others, and it makes little difference whether we are a hand or a foot, as long as we recognize that we are an important part of Christ's body.

The example of Shadrack and friends is one of great courage, courage which enabled them to obey God in the face of certain death. Their courage, however, came from their knowledge of God, not from their own strength of character. They may well have been as timid as Mark for all we know; yet they understood that their God has complete control over their lives, and this assurance gave them the courage to obey.

This week we will see how three young men were sure of one thing—that God is Lord of heaven and earth—and this assurance led them to accomplish great things.

ACTIVITIES

Choose one of the activities below.

BIRTHDAY LINEUP Without talking have the group arrange themselves in order of their birthdays (not age).

LOSING CONTROL Spin a person around many times. Then have that person navigate an obstacle course holding a stick or bat to the forehead with the other end just off the floor.

ICEBREAKERS

Choose one or two of these icebreakers.

››› Where is the hottest place you've ever been?

››› What is the most exotic or unusual musical instrument you've ever played?

››› What is the biggest statue you've ever seen? Who or what was it of?

SCRIPTURE READING

Read the following passage from
Daniel 3:1-28

READER ONE. [1] King Nebuchadnezzar made an image of gold, ninety feet high and nine feet wide, and set it up on the plain of Dura in the province of Babylon. ... [4] Then the herald loudly proclaimed, "This is what you are commanded to do, O peoples, nations and men of every language: [5] As soon as you hear the sound of the horn, flute, zither, lyre, harp, pipes and all kinds of music, you must fall down and worship the image of gold that King Nebuchadnezzar has set up. [6] Whoever does not fall down and worship will immediately be thrown into a blazing furnace."

READER TWO. [7] Therefore, as soon as they heard the sound of the horn, flute, zither, lyre, harp and all kinds of music, all the peoples, nations and men of every language fell down and worshiped the image of gold that King Nebuchadnezzar had set up. [8] At this time some astrologers came forward and denounced the Jews. [9] They said to King Nebuchadnezzar, "O king, live forever! [10] You have issued a decree, [11] ... that whoever does not fall down and worship will be thrown into a blazing furnace. [12] But there are some Jews whom you have set over the affairs of the province of Babylon—Shadrach, Meshach and Abednego—who pay no attention to you, O king. They neither serve your gods nor worship the image of gold you have set up."

READER THREE. [13] Furious with rage, Nebuchadnezzar summoned Shadrach, Meshach and Abednego. So these men were brought before the king, [14] and Nebuchadnezzar said to them, "Is it true, Shadrach, Meshach and Abednego, that you do not serve my gods or worship the image of gold I have set up? [15] Now when you hear the sound of the horn, flute, zither, lyre, harp, pipes and all kinds of music, if you are ready to fall down and worship the image I made, very good. But if you do not worship it, you will be thrown immediately into a blazing furnace. Then what god will be able to rescue you from my hand?"

READER FOUR. [16] Shadrach, Meshach and Abednego replied to the king, "O Nebuchadnezzar, we do not need to defend ourselves before you in this matter. [17] If we are thrown into the blazing furnace, the God we serve is able to save us from it, and he will rescue us from your hand, O king. [18] But even if he does not, we want you to know, O king, that we will not serve your gods or worship the image of gold you have set up." ¹⁹ Then Nebuchadnezzar was furious with Shadrach, Meshach and Abednego, and his attitude toward them changed. He ordered the furnace heated seven times hotter than usual ²⁰ and commanded some of the strongest soldiers in his army to tie up Shadrach, Meshach and Abednego and throw them into the blazing furnace. ²¹ So these men ... were bound and thrown into the blazing furnace. ²² The king's command was so urgent and the furnace so hot that the flames of the fire killed the soldiers who took up Shadrach, Meshach and Abednego, ²³ and these three men, firmly tied, fell into the blazing furnace.

READER FIVE. ²⁴ Then King Nebuchadnezzar leaped to his feet in amazement and asked his advisers, "Weren't there three men that we tied up and threw into the fire?" They replied, "Certainly, O king." ²⁵ He said, "Look! I see four men walking around in the fire, unbound and unharmed, and the fourth looks like a son of the gods." ²⁶ Nebuchadnezzar then approached the opening of the blazing furnace and shouted, "Shadrach, Meshach and Abednego, servants of the Most High God, come out! Come here!"

READER SIX. So Shadrach, Meshach and Abednego came out of the fire, ²⁷ and the satraps, prefects, governors and royal advisers crowded around them. They saw that the fire had not harmed their bodies, nor was a hair of their heads singed; their robes were not scorched, and there was no smell of fire on them.
²⁸ Then Nebuchadnezzar said, "Praise be to the God of Shadrach, Meshach and Abednego, who has sent his angel and rescued his servants! They trusted in him and defied the king's command and were willing to give up their lives rather than serve or worship any god except their own God."

Daniel 3:1-28

DISCUSSION QUESTIONS

Select four or five questions from the head and heart sections, and/or make up your own.

››› Why do Shadrach and his friends refuse to bow down to the king's giant statue?

››› What difference would it make if they had bowed down?

>>> Why do the young men not even try to defend themselves before the king?

>>> Where do these men find their courage?

>>> What exactly are these young men sure of? What are they unsure of? Which is more important?

>>> What things in life are you unsure of? What are you sure of?

>>> How does this assurance help you find significance and security?

>>> In what way was obedience to God necessary for Shadrach and friends to find courage?

>>> If you had been in their place, what would you have done? Would you have been so sure of God's power?

>>> How can this assurance of God's faithfulness affect your life in the coming week?

CARING TIME

Use these questions and/or make up your own.

>>> Are you sure that God loves you? That He will always be faithful to you?

>>> Do you lack courage when faced with some areas of obedience? How can this group help?

>>> From these studies, what would you say are the most important things for you to accomplish in life?

4 peoples, nations, and men of every language. Shadrach and the others have great courage in refusing to bow down, since the whole world was doing it.

15 what god will be able to rescue you. This is the root of the challenge facing these men—the king has set himself up as equal to God. The young men are quite sure that the king is not equal to their God, though they may be less confident that He will save them from the flames. But it is their assurance that they act on, not their misgivings, and this is the secret of courage.

16 we do not need to defend ourselves. They are completely confident that God is watching them, and that He will defend them as He sees fit. Their only job is to obey Him and leave the rest to Him.

18 we will not serve your gods. The young friends are determined to obey God, yet they have also counted the cost. It may well cost them their lives, but they are completely sure that God will be faithful to them. This assurance gives them the courage to be faithful to Him.

25 I see four men. God does not disappoint them. In fact, He has been there all along, watching over His servants. As a result of God's intervention in this situation, all those around them saw the reality of the one true God. Shadrach and friends would have cheated others of a knowledge of God if they had not acted with courage and assurance.From these studies, what would you say are the most important things for you to accomplish in life?

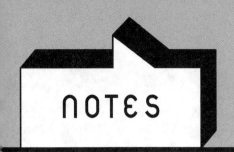

NOTES

NOTES